Rebuilding the Wall
Lessons from Nehemiah

Vanessa M. Wilson, J.D.

Grants and Proposal Writing for
Faith Based Organizations 2014

Legal Information

ISBN: 978-0-9798625-6-4

Source of images: www.fotolia.com

www.vanessawilson.info
vanessa@vanessawilson.info
Voice: (888)530-4485
Fax: (609)751-9385

"There is still money on the planet, so follow the cloud."
Vanessa M. Wilson, J.D.

"Sometimes the cloud would settle only overnight, and they would march when the cloud ascended in the morning. Whether it was day or night, they would march when the cloud ascended. Whether it was two days, or a month, or a long time, the Israelites would camp so long as the cloud lingered on the dwelling and settled on it. They wouldn't march. But when it ascended, they would march. They camped at the Lord's command and they marched at the Lord's command. They followed the Lord's direction according to the Lord's command through Moses."
Numbers 9:21-23

This Study Guide and Workbook is the companion outline for **Rebuilding the Wall - Lessons from Nehemiah Grants and Proposal Writing for Faith Based Organization Parts One and Two"**, developed and conducted by Vanessa M. Wilson, J.D.
The 2014 edition contains new 501(c)(3) information effective July 1, 2014.

Contents

vanessa@vanessawilson.info

vanessa@vanessawilson.info

Welcome

"I believe that accountability can only be achieved with strategic thinking and planning, periodic self-assessment - and absolute transparency in communicating our progress toward our goals." Vartan Gregorian.

Introductions

- The CrossWalk Group, LLC
  cross·walk (krôs'wôk') - a specially designated path where something can be crossed to get from one side to the other.

- The mission of The CrossWalk Group is to empower individuals and organizations to do what they do best by providing high quality training and services that build knowledge, infrastructure and capacity.

Vanessa M. Wilson, J.D. Presenter

- Dr. Wilson has written for and been awarded public and private grants and contracts. She has also served member of the grants review teams and bid evaluation committees in both the public and private sectors. This presentation and the information contained in this ***Study Guide and Workbook*** is her intellectual property combined with resources that she has gathered during many years of proposal writing and review. She is a founding principal of the Crosswalk Group, LLC. One of her goals is to provide information and education to people who are committed to serving others.

Participant introductions

- Name
- Organization
- What is your role in your organization
- What do you want to leave with

Nehemiah 6:15-16

> *"So the wall was finished on the twenty-fifth day of the month Elul, in fifty-two days. And when all our enemies heard of it, all the nations around us were afraid and fell greatly in their own esteem; for they perceived that this work had been accomplished with the help of our God."*

Nehemiah 1, 2

- The foundation of a good proposal/project
- Vision 1
- Mission 1
- Statement of need 1:3; 2:3
- Request for proposal 2:4
- Proposal 2:5-7
- Timeline 2:6
- Collaboration 2:7
- Budget 2:8
- **Grant** 2:8
- Confidentiality statement 2:12; 2:16
- Needs assessment 2:11-15
- Mission statement 2:17
- Acknowledgment of support 2:18
- Implementation plan 3
- Documentation 3
- Opposition 4
- Integrity 5:14-19
- Mission accomplished 7

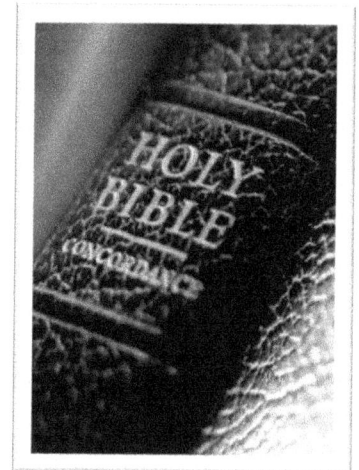

Grants

"Words - so innocent and powerless as they are, as standing in a dictionary, how potent for good and evil they become in the hands of one who knows how to combine them." Nathaniel Hawthorne

What is a Grant?

"Bounty, contribution, gift, or subsidy (in cash or kind) bestowed by a government or other organization (called the grantor) for specified purposes to an eligible recipient (called the grantee). Grants are usually conditional upon certain qualifications as to the use, maintenance of specified standards, or a proportional contribution by the grantee or other grantor(s)."
Source: http://www.businessdictionary.com/definition/grant.html

What is a Grant?

- Individuals
- Scholarships
- Fellowships
- Self-development
- Professorship
- Book awards
- Housing
- Other

Grant Makers

- Individuals
- Foundations
- Government
- Local
- State
- Federal
- Community based organizations [CBO]
- Faith based organizations [FBO]
- Other

Alphabet Soup

RFP	RFQ	RFA	NGO	RFB	FOA
AFB	FBO	CEO	CFO	CIO	MOU
FDP	PDF	CCR	GSA	FY	TIN [EIN]
OMB	CFR	CO	FOIA	OPRA	HUD
DUNS	SAM	BAFO	FSR	JIT	HR/HI

Grants and Other $$$

- Grants
  - Restricted
  - Unrestricted
  - Government
  - Discretionary
  - Nondiscretionary
  - Block grants
- Contracts for
  - Service provision
  - Product delivery

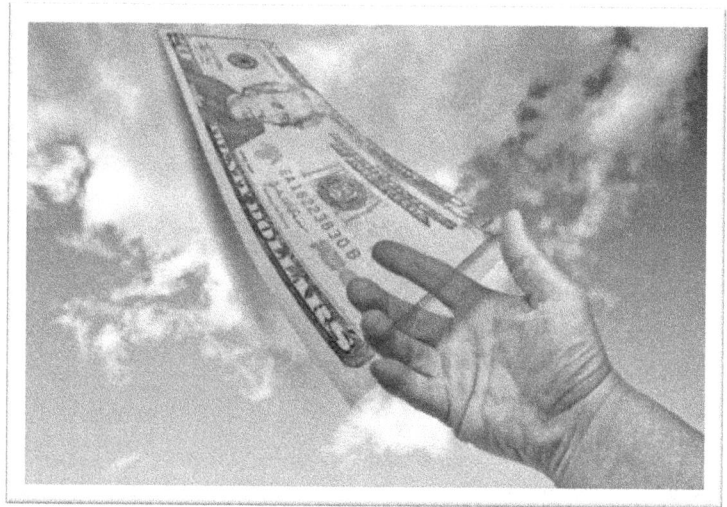

Organizational Structure

"Then he said, "Give to Caesar what belongs to Caesar and to God what belongs to God."
Matthew 22:21

Legal Formation

- Organizations must be a legal entity
- Profit vs. Nonprofit
- Nonprofit
  - 501(c)(s)
  - 1023-EZ
  - http://www.irs.gov/pub/irs-pdf/i1023ez.pdf

Legal Formation - All

- Tax payer identification number/Employer identification number
- D-U-N-S number
- http://fedgov.dnb.com/webform/displayHomePage.do
- Central Contractor Registration (C.C.R.)
- The System for Award Management (S.A.M) is a free web site that consolidates the capabilities you used to find in CCR/FedReg, ORCA, and EPLS. Future phases of SAM will add the capabilities of other systems used in Federal procurement and awards processes.

501(c)(3)

- Federal
- State requirements
- Formation
- Infrastructure
- By-laws
- Board of directors
- Annual meetings
- Records
- Policies and procedures
- Formation can be
  - Time consuming
  - Detailed driven
  - Mistakes can cost time and dollars

Board of Directors

- Treasury
- Talent
- Time
- Technology
- Transparency

Infrastructure

- Mission
- Vision
- Values
- Strategic Plan
- Financial Plan
  - Budget
  - Fundraising

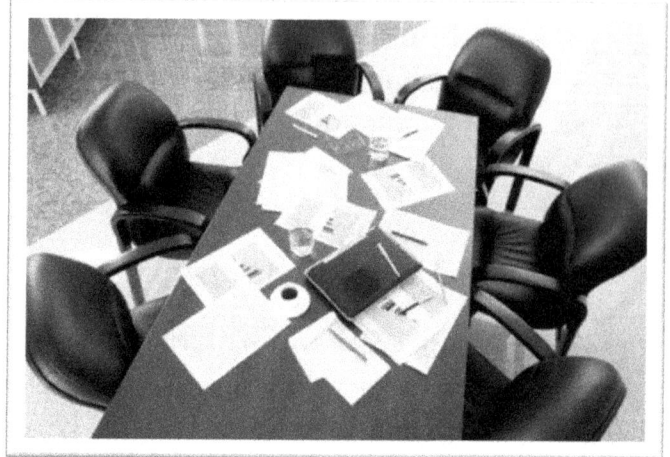

Organization Cycle

- Start
  - Define the mission
  - Compelling case statement
  - Elevator speech
  - Quality statement
  -
- Grow
  - Create SMART objectives
    - **S**pecific
    - **M**easurable
    - **A**chievable
    - **R**ealistic/**R**elevant
    - **T**ime sensitive
  - Service/product delivery
- Mature (Sustain)
  - Self-sustaining
  - Team building (Internal)
  - Collaboration (External)
- Decline or Reinvent
  - Assess and Act
  - Internal assessment + External feedback = Overall organizational performance

Planning

"Write a vision, and make it plain upon a tablet so that a runner can read it. There is still a vision for the appointed time; it testifies to the end; it does not deceive." Habakkuk 2:2-3

SWOT

- Strengths
- Weaknesses
- Opportunities
- Threats

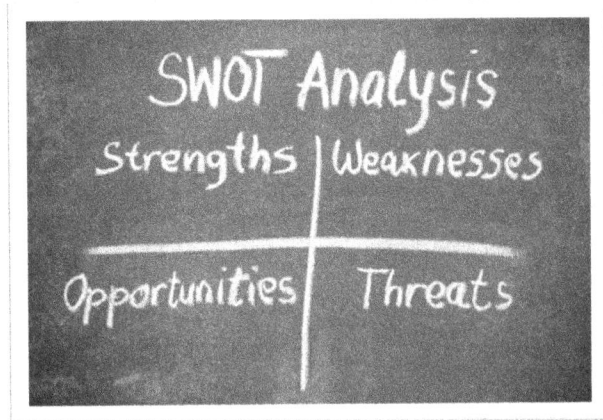

SLEPT

- Social
- Legal
- Economic
- Political
- Technology

Appreciative Inquiry

- Discover
- Dream
- Design
- Destiny (Deliver)

SOAR

- Strengths
- Opportunities
- Aspirations
- Results

Logic Model

Program: Goal:					
INPUTS	ACTIVITIES		OUTCOMES (Deliverables)		
What we invest	What we do	Who we reach	Why this project		
			Short-term	Intermediate	Long-term
Assumptions			External Factors (Influences)		

Successful Fundraising

> *"Donors don't give to institutions. They invest in ideas and people in whom they believe."*
>
> *G.T. Smith*

Steps to Successful Fundraising

- Involvement
  - Community
  - Government
  - Grant Makers
  - Corporations
  - Banks
- Visibility
  - Branding
  - No negative press
  - Web presence
  - Social Media
- Efficiency
  - Resourcefulness
  - Ethical
  - Timely
- Effective
  - Did you achieve stated goals?
  - Do you have positive outcomes?
- Stability
  - Consistency in mission and operations
- Integrity
  - Transparency
- Conduct Effective Research
  - Who are the customers/constituents?
  - What does the customer/constituent need?
- Who or what is the competition?
  - What are the gaps in the market/service provision?
  - Do customers/constituents like [need/use] product/service?

Grant Application

"Proofread carefully to see if you any words out."   *Author Unknown*

Eligibility Requirements
- Applicant
- Beneficiary
- Required documents
  - EIN
  - DUNS
  - State business registration certification
  - Bylaws
  - Board of directors
  - License
  - Records

Grantor
- Government
  - Federal
  - State
  - Local
    - County
    - Municipality
- Private
  - Corporations
  - Foundations
  - Individuals

Contact Information
- Applicant
  - CEO
  - CFO/Accountant
  - Board of directors
- Grantor
  - Grant administrator
  - Procurement officer
  - CFDA Number – Catalogue of Federal Domestic Assistance
    - https://www.cfda.gov/
  - Funding Opportunity Number
  - Funding Opportunity Competition Number

Federal Assistance

- Application Process
- Online
- On site
    - Hand deliver
    - Courier
- US postal service
    - Post mark
    - Date received
- US Federal Contractor Registration
    - https://usfederalcontractorregistration.com/index_MADR.html
    - Grants.gov
- Term
- Renewals
- Deadlines
- Selection criterion

Evaluation Criterion - Example

- Tax clearance - REQUIRED
- General provisions - REQUIRED
- Title page - REQUIRED
- Category of workers
- Training programs
- Training provider
- *Total Points 35*
- Narrative
    - Company background
    - Expected outcomes
    - If employer, commitment to hire/retain workers trained
    - If not an employer, commitment letters from employers
    - How trained workers will be rewarded
    - Leveraged resources
    - Agreement on reporting
- *Total Points 45*
- Budget: – Allowable Costs
- *Total Points 20*
- Costs identified are within NGO guidelines
- *TOTAL   100*

- Source: Competitive Notice Of Grant Opportunity, State Energy Sector Partnership (SESP) Grant For The Energy Efficiency Industries

Award Process

- How money is awarded
  - Advance
  - Reimbursement
  - Check
  - Letter of credit
  - Schedule of payment
  - Matching funds
  - Formula
- Appeal Process

Keep It Coming

- Recordkeeping
  - Staff training
  - Board training
  - Policies and procedures
  - Client/Service records
- Audits
  - Financial Audits
    - Grantor audit
      - OMB A-133
    - Independent audit
    - CPA
  - Compliance Audits
  - Operational Audits
  - Investigative Audits
  - Information Systems (IS) Audits
- Reports
  - Monthly
  - Quarterly
  - Annually
  - Interim
  - Close-out
- Program Assessments
  - Progress against goals
  - Client evaluations
  - Outcome assessment

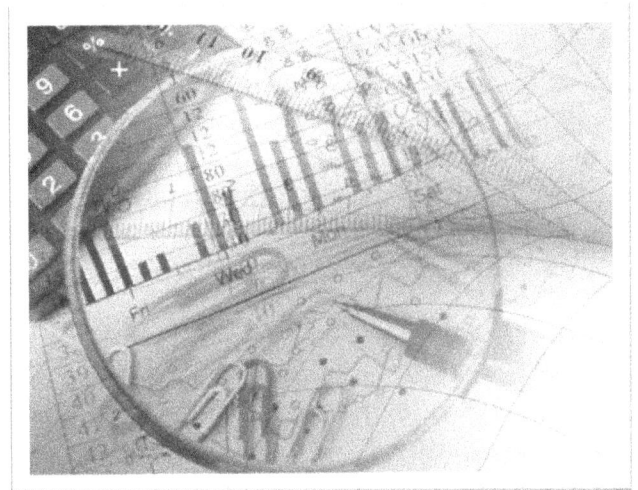

Beginning the Proposal Writing Process

"For your born writer, nothing is so healing as the realization that he has come upon the right word." Catherine Drinker Bowen

The Proposal Writing Process

- There are four main categories of proposals.
- *Note that these categories can and do overlap – proposals are unique to each situation and each organization.*
  - Technical proposal
  - Sales proposals
  - Cost proposal
  - Professional service proposal

About Requests for Proposals

- A 'Request for Proposal' is a document issued by a funder requesting proposals for a particular project. Information commonly requested via an 'RFP' can include:
  - Organizational background
  - Organization's experience with the requested product or service
  - Solution details
  - Project timeline and budget
  - Customer/client references

Performing a Needs Analysis

- A good needs analysis must answer four questions:
  - Who are the "customers" (readers & end-users) of the proposal?
  - What do they want or need?
  - What do they currently have as a solution?
- What can we offer?

Preparing an Outline

- A General Format
  - Cover Letter
  - Title Page
  - Proprietary Notice
  - Table of Contents
  - Executive Summary
  - Introduction
  - Body
  - Summary and Conclusions
  - Bibliography
- Special Sections
  - Table of Figures (if there are a lot of illustrations in the proposal)
  - Statement of understanding
  - Organizational history
  - Summary of writer's credentials

- o Proposed project timeline
- o Cost-benefit analysis
- o Benefits summary
- o Scientific method
- o Budget
- o Budget narrative
- o Specific project elements, such as proposed product design, marketing plan, schedule, etc.
- o Problem analysis
- o Glossary of jargon, technical terms, etc.

Creating a Framework - Example

- Cover letter
- Title page
- Proprietary Notice
- Table of Contents
- Executive Summary
- Introduction
- Organization History
- Need Statement
- Analysis
- Solution
- Summary and conclusions
- Bibliography

Table of Contents

"Words - so innocent and powerless as they are, as standing in a dictionary, how potent for good and evil they become in the hands of one who knows how to combine them."
Nathaniel Hawthorne

Proposal

- Executive summary
- Project summary
- Problem statement
- Goals and objectives
- Project description
- Management plan
- Budget
  - Budget justification (Narrative)
- Continuation (Sustainability) plan
- Evaluation plan
- Dissemination plan
- Key personnel biosketches
- Timeline
- Bibliography
- Appendices
  - Letters of support
  - Letters of collaboration
  - Board of directors
  - Organization chart
  - Other

Finding Facts

> *"Research is to see what everybody else has seen, and to think what nobody else has thought." Albert Szent-Gyorgyi*

Identifying Resources

- Where do you look for facts?
    - Observing and interviewing
    - Organization employees/community residents
    - Organization documents and reports
    - Consultants if they are available to you
    - Industry experts (with credentials for their expertise)
    - Reports from accredited organizations
    - Scientific studies
    - Publications such as journals and magazines
    - Books

Using the Internet as a Resource

- Some tips
    - Use information from accredited, reliable organizations
    - Go directly to primary sources to for information
    - Use the Internet to find offline resources

Organizing Your Information

- Some other methods include
    - Chronological order (most recent to oldest, or vice versa)
    - By level of detail (simplest to most complex, or vice versa)
    - By importance
    - Separated by pros and cons, with a conclusion at the end
    - By offering a question and then an answer

Writing Skills, Part One

"The role of a writer is not to say what we all can say, but what we are unable to say."
Anaïs Nin

Spelling and Grammar

- Remember basic rules
- Proposals should usually use the third person
- Acronyms and texting slang do not belong in a proposal
- Know what errors you commonly make - make an effort to correct them
- Writing well takes practice
- Invest in at least one good grammar reference resource
- Make use of available tools, such as spell check, dictionaries, thesauri and people directories
- If you are stuck on a sentence, try reading it out loud
- Always re-read your work

Working with Words

- Proposals should be objective rather than subjective (No first person "I")
- Include the appropriate level of detail in each sentence and paragraph
- Check to see if you have said the same thing in different ways
- To see if you have used the right word, try substituting synonyms for your chosen word
- Be very careful when using jargon, slang and acronyms

Constructing Sentences

- Simple: A single idea expressed with one subject and one verb
- Compound: Two ideas expressed together
- Complex: A single idea, with a dependent idea

Persuasive Writing

- Consistency
- Reciprocity
- Social Validation
- Likability
- Authority
- Scarcity

Mastering Voice

- There are two voices in writing
  - Active voice - the writer is doing something
    - Example: "I bounced the ball."
  - Passive voice - something is being done
    - Example: "The ball was bounced."

Writing Skills, Part Two
"The worst enemy to creativity is self-doubt." *Sylvia Plath*

Creating Paragraphs

- A basic paragraph is simply a collection of sentences. A good paragraph, however, is much more than that.
    - It has a beginning, middle, and an end.
    - It focuses on one theme or idea.
    - It ties to the paragraphs before and after it to help build to a logical conclusion.
- Typically, paragraphs are structured like this:
    - The beginning should state the key theme in one sentence.
    - The middle should provide support for the key theme in three to five sentences.
    - The end should summarize the key theme in one sentence. It can also provide solutions, give answers or transition to the next paragraph.

Creating Strong Transitions

- However
- Also
- Likewise
- Consequently
- Previously
- On the other hand
- In conclusion
- To illustrate
- In contrast

Building to Conclusions

- There should be several levels of conclusions in your proposal
    - Mini-conclusion at the end of each paragraph, tying the main points together and transitioning to the next paragraph
    - Conclusion paragraph at the end of each part of a section, tying all the paragraphs in that section together
- Conclusion paragraph at the end of each major section, tying all the sections together

Writing the Proposal

"How do I know what I think until I see what I say?" E. M. Forster

Educating the Evaluator

- Statement of understanding
- Benefits analysis
- Organizational impact statement

Ghosting the Competition

- When writing the proposal
  - Make sure to include alternate solutions
  - Show why they are not appropriate
- Whenever possible
  - highlight the deficiencies in other approaches to the problem
  - show how your proposed solution does not have those areas of weakness
- Using illustrations
  - Some overall tips for diagrams:
    - Only use an illustration if it helps to convey your point
    - Make sure to use the proper type of illustration (chart)
    - Each illustration should convey one major point
    - Where possible, construct diagrams using a computer (professionalism)
    - Number each sequentially
    - Include a Table of Figures at the beginning of your proposal

Checking for Readability

"Never use a 50-cent word when a 10-cent word will do." Unknown

Checking for Clarity

- Use the following checklist to help make sure your writing will be clear to your readers.
- Have I used words with their correct meaning and in their correct context?
- Have I used punctuation appropriately?
- Have I used jargon or slang? Should I explain myself?
- Have I used the active voice wherever possible?
- Are my sentences clearly constructed?
- Do my paragraphs transition well?
- Have I primarily used the third person?
- Does each paragraph have a logical beginning, middle, and end, focused around one idea?
- Does each paragraph, sub-section, and section tie back to the goal statement?

Reading for Your Audience

- As a final check for clarity, try to anticipate any questions that your audience may have. Things to check for include
- Have you used jargon that needs to be explained?
- Have you written at an appropriate level?
- Are all sections written for the correct audience?
- Have you provided enough background information?
- Do your supporting points clearly lead to a conclusion?

Using the Readability Index

- Count the number of words.
- Count the number of sentences.
- Divide the number of words by the number of sentences. This will give you the average sentence length.
- Count the number of words with three or more syllables. Exclude the following words: proper names, jargon, compound words, words with a suffix (such as -ing, -es, -ed, etc.).
- Divide the number of polysyllabic words by the number of words in the passage. Multiply by 100. This is the percentage of complex words in the passage.
- Add the average sentence length to the percentage of complex words.
- Multiply this total by 0.4 to get your fog factor.

Proofreading and Editing

- Proofreading Like a pro
  - Set up an environment conducive to editing, with good lighting, minimal distractions the tools you need.
  - Make a conscious effort to read slowly
  - Read the document several times.
  - Read it out loud
  - Reading in the opposite order: from the bottom to the top of the page, and from the end to the beginning of a paragraph.
  - If you're not sure what a word means look it up.
  - Expect to find mistakes.

"There is no great writing, only great rewriting."   **Justice Brandeis**

Editing Techniques

- Editing is different from proofreading
  - Proofreading focuses on spelling and grammar
  - Editing looks at the clarity, accuracy, and consistency of the document as a whole
- Checking the Facts
  - Validity of quotes from people
  - Mathematical calculations
  - Presentation, analysis, and interpretation of studies
  - Phrasing of statistics
    - use of words like always, exactly, never
  - Check web sites and links

The Power of Peer Review

- Grants review team
  - Internal
    - Finance
    - Human Resources
    - Public Relations/ Marketing
    - Program personnel
    - Other
  - External
    - Collaborators
    - Partners
    - College professor
- Incorporate feedback into the proposal as necessary

Adding the Final Touches

> *"For me, writing is hard work. I always look forward to drawing the pictures."*
> *Marc Brown*

Word Processing Tips

Respect organizational policies and any requirements set out by the grantor. Their rules supersede anything in this presentation.

- Use a maximum of two font faces
  - one for heading
  - one for the body
- Establish a consistent formatting scheme throughout the document
- Use common fonts
  - Times New Roman, Calibri, Arial, or Verdana
- Use font effects sparingly or not at all
- Use formatting built in to the software

Creating the Final Package - Achieving a Professional Look and Feel

- Use plenty of white space
- Give your proposal a title and create a title page (specified by grantor process)
- Have all signatures in same color (blue) ink
- Use consistent headers and footers that include page numbers
- Ensure that all components match
- Make sure that all sections are present and that all pages are in order
- Include a blank page at the end
- Simple, professional binding, such as spiral binding or an elegant three-ring binder can make a big impact
- Turn in requisite copies
- Follow the submission guidelines; cross check to ensure adherence
- Keep printed copies clean and dry
- Corrections
  - make them on the computer
  - print new copies
  - no handwritten notes with arrows

GRANTS

JUST AHEAD

Appendix

Alphabet Soup – Commonly Used Acronyms

AFB – Advertisement for Bids
B2B – Business to Business
B2C – Business to Consumer
B2G – Business to Government
CAGE – Commercial And Government Entity Code
CCR – Central Contractor Registration
CDBG – Community Development Block Grant
CEO – Chief Executive Officer
CFO – Chief Financial Officer
CFR – Code of Federal Regulation
CFDA – Catalog of Federal Domestic Assistance
CHRO – Chief Human Resources Officer
CIO – Chief Information Officer
CO – Certifying Officer
CDBG – Community Development Block Grant
CSBG – Community Services Block Grant
D&B – Dun & Bradstreet
DUNS – Data Universal Numbering System (D&B)
EPLS – Excluded Parties List System
FBO – Federal Business Opportunity
FDP – Federal Demonstration Project
FOA – Federal Opportunity Announcement
FOIA – Freedom of Information Act
FSR – Financial Status Reports
FSRS – Federal Funding Accountability and Transparency Act
FTE – Full time equivalent
FY – Fiscal Year
GSA – US General Services Administration
HBCU – Historically Black Colleges & Universities
HUD – U.S. Housing and Urban Development
MBDA – Minority Business Development
MBE – Minority Business Enterprise
MOU – Memorandum of Understanding
NGO – Notice of Grant Opportunity
OMB – Office of Management and Budget
O*NET – Occupational Information Network
OPRA – Open Public Records Act
PDF –Portable Document Format
RFA – Request for Applications
RFB – Request for Bids
RFP – Request for Proposals
RFQ – Request for Quote
ROI – Return on Investment

SAM – System for Award Management
S2S – System to System
TIN [EIN] – Tax Identification number – [Employer Identification Number]
UBIT – Unrelated Business Income Tax

Writing Work Book

Full legal name of organization

_____

If the organization has not started, please provide three alternative names for the organization

_____

_____

_____

Name of CEO/Founder(s)

_____

_____

_____

Names of members of the Board of Directors

_____

_____

_____

_____

_____

_____

Names of the Leadership/Management Team

_____

_____

_____

_____

_____

_____

Number of staff Full-time _____   Part-time _____   Other _____

How long have you been in existence? _____

What is the organization's line of business? (Include Standard Industrial Classification (SIC) Code and North American Industry Classification System (NAICS)?)

_____

_____

_____

_____

_____

_____

_____

What is your Employer Identification Number (EIN) or Taxpayer Identification Number (TIN)?

_____

What is your DUNS Number?

_____

Are you registered with the Central Contractor Registration (CCR)? ☐ Yes ☐ No

What services and/or products does your organization offer?

_____

_____

_____

_____

_____

_____

_____

_____

_____

_____

What does your business specialize in?/ What unique services does your business offer?

_____
_____
_____
_____
_____
_____
_____
_____
_____
_____
_____
_____
_____

What other lines of business is your organization or affiliated entities involved in, if any?

_____
_____
_____
_____
_____
_____
_____
_____

Vision

_____
_____
_____
_____
_____
_____
_____
_____
_____
_____

Mission

_____
_____
_____
_____
_____
_____
_____
_____
_____
_____

Core Values

_____
_____
_____
_____
_____
_____
_____
_____
_____
_____

Compelling Case Statement

_____
_____
_____
_____
_____
_____
_____
_____
_____
_____

Elevator Pitch

_____

_____

_____

_____

_____

_____

_____

_____

_____

Reason for funding

_____

_____

_____

_____

_____

_____

_____

_____

_____

_____

Business Structure

☐ C Corporation   ☐ Limited Liability Company

☐ S Corporation   ☐ General Partnership

☐ Limited Partnership   ☐ Sole Proprietorship

☐ Non-profit   ☐ Other

If you checked "Other," please explain.

_____

_____

_____

_____

Is the corporation an International, National or Regional corporation?

☐ Yes ☐ No

If you checked "Yes", please explain.

_____

_____

_____

_____

_____

Is your organization a franchise, a division or an affiliate of any other organization?

☐ Yes ☐ No

If you checked Yes", please explain.

_____

_____

_____

_____

_____

About Your Organization's Financial Status

Last full year's gross revenues $_____

5-year revenue goal $_____

List your assets

_____

_____

_____

_____

_____

Do you currently have or do you plan to bid for or apply for public contracts?

☐ Yes ☐ No

Are you bondable?

☐ Yes ☐ No

The Nonprofit Checklist

The formation of a legally recognized nonprofit organization is a detailed and tedious task of document gathering. The maintenance of the organization also requires ongoing compliance, recordkeeping and accurate accounting. The checklist below will you gather the necessary documents for a complete application. Any item with an asterisk (*) is mandatory for the application to be submitted. If you have questions or would like to schedule an appointment, feel free to contact me at vanessa@vanessawilson.info *or call (888)530-4485. Thank you.*

Legal names, address, telephone number, fax number, e-mail and web site of your organization. If your organization's name has been officially changed by an amendment to your organizing instruments, you should also attach a conformed copy of that amendment to your application.*

Name, address and title of Board members (at least three).*

Organizing or Enabling documents such as Articles of Incorporation (and the Certificate of Incorporation, if available), Articles of Association, Trust Indenture, Constitution, etc.*

Amendments to Articles of Incorporation in chronological order.

Bylaws or other rules of operation and amendments.*

Employer Identification number. *

Board policies, including :

"Conflict of Interest" policy for officers and board members.*

Policy regarding business income unrelated to you non-profit purpose.

Documentation of nondiscriminatory policy for schools.

Mission and vision and statements.*

Description of activities including:*

A full description of the proposed activities of your organization,

Comprehensive fundraising plan including each of the fundraising activities of the organization and a narrative description of anticipated receipts and contemplated expenditures.

Include the standards, criteria, procedures, or other means that your organization adopted or planned for carrying out those activities.

Financial data including:*

Financial statements showing your receipts and expenditures and a balance sheet for the current year and the 4 preceding years (or for the number of years your organization was in existence, if less than 4 years).

For each accounting period, you must describe the sources of your receipts and the nature of your expenditures.

If you have not yet begun operations, or have operated for less than 1 year, a proposed budget for 3 full accounting periods and a current statement of assets and liabilities will be acceptable.

Other information may be requested by the IRS including but not limited to:

Representative copies of advertising placed

Copies of publications, such as magazines

Distributed written material used for expressing views on proposed legislation, and

Copies of leases, contracts, or agreements into which your organization has entered.

User fee payment placed in envelope.*

For Faith-based organizations (Information excerpted from IRS publication Form 1023)
"To determine whether an organization meets the religious purposes test of section 501(c)(3), the IRS maintains two basic guidelines.

That the particular religious beliefs of the organization are truly and sincerely held.

That the practices and rituals associated with the organization's religious belief or creed are not illegal or contrary to clearly defined public policy.

Therefore, your group (or organization) may not qualify for treatment as an exempt religious organization for tax purposes if its actions, as contrasted with its beliefs, are contrary to well established and clearly defined public policy. If there is a clear showing that the beliefs (or doctrines) are sincerely held by those professing them, the IRS will not question the religious nature of those beliefs.

Churches. Although a church, its integrated auxiliaries, or a convention or association of churches is not required to file Form 1023 to be exempt from federal income tax or to receive tax deductible contributions, the organization may find it advantageous to obtain recognition of exemption. [Emphasis added]In this event, you should submit information showing that your organization is a church, synagogue, association or convention of churches, religious order, or religious organization that is an integral part of a church, and that it is engaged in carrying out the function of a church.

In determining whether an admittedly religious organization is also a church, the IRS does not accept any and every assertion that the organization is a church. Because beliefs and practices vary so widely, there is no single definition of the word church for tax purposes. The IRS considers the facts and circumstances of each organization applying for church status."

Questionnaire for Churches

Do you have a written creed, statement of faith, or summary of beliefs? If "Yes," attach copies of relevant documents.

Do you have a form of worship? If "Yes," describe your form of worship.

Do you have a formal code of doctrine and discipline? If "Yes," describe your code of doctrine and discipline.

Do you have a distinct religious history? If "Yes," describe your religious history.

Do you have a literature of your own? If "Yes," describe your literature.

Describe the organization's religious hierarchy or ecclesiastical government.

Do you have regularly scheduled religious services? If "Yes," describe the nature of the services and provide representative copies of relevant literature such as church bulletins.

What is the average attendance at your regularly scheduled religious services?

Do you have an established place of worship? If "Yes," state the location, form of ownership, include lease, mortgage, etc.

Do you own the property where you have an established place of worship?

Do you have an established congregation or other regular membership group?

How many members do you have?

Do you have a process by which an individual becomes a member? If "Yes," describe the process.

If you have members, do your members have voting rights, rights to participate in religious functions, or other rights? If "Yes," describe the rights your members have.

May your members be associated with another denomination or church?

Are all of your members part of the same family?

Do you conduct baptisms, weddings, funerals, etc.?

Do you have a school for the religious instruction of the young?

Do you have a minister or religious leader? If "Yes," describe this person's role and explain whether the minister or religious leader was ordained, commissioned, or licensed after a prescribed course of study.

Do you have schools for the preparation of your ordained ministers or religious leaders?

Is your minister or religious leader also one of your officers, directors, or trustees?

Do you ordain, commission, or license ministers or religious leaders? If "Yes," describe the requirements for ordination, commission, or licensure.

Are you part of a group of churches with similar beliefs and structures? If "Yes," explain. Include the name of the group of churches.

Do you issue church charters? If "Yes," describe the requirements for issuing a charter.

Did you pay a fee for a church charter? If "Yes," attach a copy of the charter.

Do you have other information you believe should be considered regarding your status as a church? If "Yes," explain.

Tips for successful management of a nonprofit organization

✓ Open a bank account in the name of the organization. Do not co-mingle funds.

✓ Find an accountant, who is knowledgeable in nonprofit accounting, to set up a basic bookkeeping system.

✓ Find an insurance agent. You may need liability insurance, property insurance, and advice about staff issues such as worker's compensation, health and life insurance benefits, and more.

✓ Find a nonprofit management professional to help with grant writing, human resources, volunteer management, program development, and other nonprofit concerns.

✓ Obtain a mail permit from your local post office for a discount on bulk mailings.

✓ Find out about unemployment and workers compensation insurance requirements from your state.

Federal Agencies the Provide Grants

The Department of Health and Human Services is the Grants.gov program's managing partner, and allows access to the 26 federal grant-making agencies available through this convenient E-Government initiative. Below are the links to those agency websites. If you would like to learn more about grants specific to these agencies.....

Agency for International Development

The Agency for International Development is an independent federal government agency that provides economic and humanitarian assistance in more than 100 countries to ensure a better future for us all.

Corporation for National and Community Service [EXIT Disclaimer]

The Corporation for National and Community Service is the nation's largest grant-maker supporting service and volunteering. Through Senior Corps, AmeriCorps and Learn and Serve America programs, the Corporation is a catalyst for change and offers every American a chance to contribute through service and volunteering.

Department of Agriculture

Established in 1862, the Department of Agriculture serves all Americans through anti-hunger efforts, stewardship of nearly 200 million acres of national forest and rangelands, and through product safety and conservation efforts. The USDA opens markets for American farmers and ranchers and provides food for needy people around the world.

Department of Commerce

The Department of Commerce fosters and promotes the nation's economic development and technological advancement through vigilance in international trade policy, domestic business policy and growth, and promoting economic progress at all levels.

Department of Defense

The Department of Defense provides the military forces needed to deter war and protect the security of the United States through five major areas: peacekeeping and war-fighting efforts, Homeland Security, evacuation and humanitarian causes.

Department of Education

The Department of Education ensures equal access to education and promotes educational excellence through coordination, management and accountability in federal education programs. The Department works to supplement and complement educational efforts on all levels, encouraging increased involvement by the public, parents and students.

Department of Energy

The Department of Energy's goal is to advance national, economic and energy security in the U.S.; to promote scientific and technological innovation in support of that and to ensure environmental cleanup of the national nuclear weapons complex.

Department of Health and Human Services

The Department of Health and Human Services is the federal government's principal agency for protecting the health of all Americans and providing essential human services, especially to those who are least able to help themselves.

Department of Homeland Security

The Department of Homeland Security has three primary missions: Prevent terrorist attacks within the United States, reduce America's vulnerability to terrorism and minimize the damage from potential attacks and natural disasters.

Department of Housing and Urban Development

The Department of Housing and Urban Development's mission is to increase homeownership, support community development and increase access to affordable housing free from discrimination. HUD fulfills this mission through high ethical standards, management and accountability, and by forming partnerships with community organizations.

Department of the Interior

The Department of the Interior protects and provides access to the Nation's natural and cultural heritage, including responsibilities to Indian tribes and island communities. Departmental goals include resource protection and usage, overseeing recreational opportunities, serving communities and excellence in management.

Department of Justice

The Department of Justice enforces the law and defends the interest of the United States, ensuring public safety against threats foreign and domestic; providing federal leadership in preventing and controlling crime; seeking just punishment for those guilty of unlawful pursuits; and ensuring fair and impartial administration of justice for all Americans.

Department of Labor

The Department of Labor fosters and promotes the welfare of job seekers, wage earners and retirees by improving their working conditions, advancing their opportunities, protecting their retirement and health benefits and generally protecting worker rights and monitoring national economic measures.

Department of State

The Department of State strives to create a more secure, democratic and prosperous world for the benefit of the American people and the international community.

Department of Transportation

The Department of Transportation's mission is to ensure fast, safe, efficient, accessible and convenient transportation that meets vital national interests and enhances the quality of life of the American people, today and into the future.

Department of the Treasury

The Department of Treasury is a steward of United States economic and financial systems, and promotes conditions for prosperity and stability in the U.S., and encourages prosperity and stability in the rest of the world.

Department of Veterans Affairs

The Department of Veterans Affairs strives for excellence in patient care and veteran's benefits for its constituents through high quality, prompt and seamless service to United States veterans.

Environmental Protection Agency

The mission of the Environmental Protection Agency is to protect human health and the environment. Since 1970, EPA has been working for a cleaner, healthier environment for the American people.

Institute of Museum and Library Services

The Institute of Museum and Library Services is the primary source of federal support for the nation's 122,000 libraries and 17,500 museums. The Institute serves as a leader in providing services to enhance learning, sustain cultural heritage and increase civic participation.

National Aeronautics and Space Administration

The National Aeronautics and Space Administration serves as the nation's forefront of such exploration and continues to pioneer in aeronautics, exploration systems, science and space operations.

National Archives and Records Administration

The National Archives and Records Administration enables people to inspect the record of what the federal government has done, enables officials and agencies to review their actions and helps citizens hold them accountable.

National Endowment for the Arts

The National Endowment for the Arts is a public agency dedicated to supporting excellence in the arts; bringing the arts to all Americans and providing leadership in arts education. The Endowment is the largest national source of funds for the arts.

National Endowment for the Humanities

The National Endowment for the Humanities is an independent grant-making agency of the United States government dedicated to supporting research, education, preservation and public programs in the humanities.

National Science Foundation

The National Science Foundation is an independent federal agency created to promote the progress of science, to advance the national health, prosperity, and welfare and to secure the national defense. The NSF annually funds approximately 20 percent of basic, federally-supported college and university research.

Small Business Administration

The Small Business Administration maintains and strengthens the nation's economy by aiding, counseling, assisting and protecting the interests of small businesses and by helping families and businesses recover from national disasters.

Social Security Administration

The Social Security Administration advances the economic security of the nation's people through compassionate and vigilant leadership in shaping and managing America's Social Security programs.

Source: http://www.grants.gov/aboutgrants/agencies_that_provide_grants.jsp

Foundations

Top 100 U.S. Foundations by Asset Size

The list below includes the 100 largest U.S. grantmaking foundations ranked by the market value of their assets, based on the most current audited financial data in the Foundation Center's database as of April 26, 2014. Fiscal records will be updated when more recent audited financial information is obtained.

Rank	Name/(state)	Assets	As of Fiscal Year End Date
1.	Bill & Melinda Gates Foundation (WA)	$37,176,776,438	12/31/2012
2.	Ford Foundation (NY)	11,238,035,011	12/31/2012
3.	J. Paul Getty Trust(CA)	10,502,514,302	06/30/2012
4.	The Robert Wood Johnson Foundation(NJ)	9,528,568,196	12/31/2012
5.	W. K. Kellogg Foundation (MI)	8,155,292,105	08/31/2013
6.	The William and Flora Hewlett Foundation (CA)	7,735,372,000	12/31/2012
7.	Lilly Endowment Inc.(IN)	7,281,773,872	12/31/2012
8.	The David and Lucile Packard Foundation(CA)	6,299,952,716	12/31/2012
9.	The John D. and Catherine T. MacArthur Foundation (IL)	5,987,438,524	12/31/2012
10.	Gordon and Betty Moore Foundation(CA)	5,697,258,026	12/31/2012
11.	The Andrew W. Mellon Foundation(NY)	5,556,152,571	12/31/2012
12.	Bloomberg Philanthropies (NY)	4,242,746,954	12/31/2012
13.	The Leona M. and Harry B. Helmsley Charitable Trust (NY)	4,241,501,002	03/31/2013
14.	Tulsa Community Foundation (OK)	3,729,789,000	12/31/2012
15.	The Rockefeller Foundation (NY)	3,695,617,868	12/31/2012
16.	The California Endowment (CA)	3,562,148,280	03/31/2013
17.	The Kresge Foundation (MI)	3,301,625,267	12/31/2012
18.	Margaret A. Cargill Foundation (MN)	2,954,027,761	12/31/2012

19.	The Duke Endowment(NC)	2,948,446,116	12/31/2012
20.	Silicon Valley Community Foundation (CA)	2,903,166,000	12/31/2012
21.	Robert W. Woodruff Foundation, Inc. (GA)	2,841,725,477	12/31/2012
22.	Carnegie Corporation of New York (NY)	2,764,431,433	09/30/2012
23.	Foundation to Promote Open Society (NY)	2,709,320,378	12/31/2012
24.	The Annie E. Casey Foundation (MD)	2,666,068,266	12/31/2012
25.	John Templeton Foundation (PA)	2,555,855,497	12/31/2012
26.	The Susan Thompson Buffett Foundation(NE)	2,384,070,265	12/31/2012
27.	Charles Stewart Mott Foundation (MI)	2,304,865,937	12/31/2012
28.	Kimbell Art Foundation (TX)	2,254,647,166	12/31/2012
29.	Conrad N. Hilton Foundation (CA)	2,230,883,024	12/31/2012
30.	Charles and Lynn Schusterman Family Foundation (OK)	2,208,464,518	12/31/2012
31.	The New York Community Trust (NY)	2,147,925,714	12/31/2012
32.	John S. and James L. Knight Foundation(FL)	2,099,590,969	12/31/2012
33.	The Simons Foundation (NY)	2,083,631,666	12/31/2012
34.	The McKnight Foundation (MN)	2,063,472,860	12/31/2012
35.	Casey Family Programs (WA)	2,061,764,408	12/31/2012
36.	Richard King Mellon Foundation (PA)	2,060,318,008	12/31/2012
37.	The Harry and Jeanette Weinberg Foundation, Inc. (MD)	2,046,251,873	02/28/2013
38.	The William Penn Foundation (PA)	2,019,462,152	12/31/2012
39.	Walton Family Foundation, Inc. (AR)	1,999,066,369	12/31/2012
40.	The Cleveland Foundation (OH)	1,883,022,162	12/31/2012
41.	Ewing Marion Kauffman Foundation(MO)	1,880,334,000	12/31/2012
42.	The Chicago Community Trust (IL)	1,804,362,755	09/30/2012
43.	Alfred P. Sloan Foundation (NY)	1,734,238,378	12/31/2012
44.	Doris Duke Charitable Foundation (NY)	1,726,653,990	12/31/2012
45.	The James Irvine Foundation (CA)	1,675,267,930	12/31/2012

vanessa@vanessawilson.info

46. Eli & Edythe Broad Foundation (CA)	1,658,457,965	12/31/2012
47. Greater Kansas City Community Foundation (MO)	1,636,468,707	12/31/2012
48. Annenberg Foundation (CA)	1,623,162,045	12/31/2012
49. The Wyss Foundation(DC)	1,558,634,475	12/31/2012
50. Houston Endowment Inc. (TX)	1,545,616,901	12/31/2012
51. The Columbus Foundation and Affiliated Organizations (OH)	1,520,768,529	12/31/2012
52. The Oregon Community Foundation (OR)	1,487,686,157	12/31/2012
53. The Heinz Endowments (PA)	1,466,928,593	12/31/2012
54. The Wallace Foundation (NY)	1,398,955,579	12/31/2012
55. Marin Community Foundation (CA)	1,333,725,159	06/30/2012
56. California Community Foundation (CA)	1,315,930,000	06/30/2013
57. Barr Foundation (MA)	1,313,184,018	12/31/2012
58. Laura and John Arnold Foundation(TX)	1,294,738,157	12/31/2012
59. Daniels Fund (CO)	1,285,511,708	12/31/2012
60. The Starr Foundation(NY)	1,273,521,260	12/31/2012
61. The Moody Foundation (TX)	1,241,224,220	12/31/2012
62. The Brown Foundation, Inc. (TX)	1,183,267,396	06/30/2013
63. The San Francisco Foundation (CA)	1,183,262,000	06/30/2013
64. The Samuel Roberts Noble Foundation, Inc. (OK)	1,172,213,441	12/31/2012
65. George Lucas Family Foundation (CA)	1,141,488,469	12/31/2012
66. Lumina Foundation(IN)	1,137,783,686	12/31/2012
67. W. M. Keck Foundation (CA)	1,105,733,000	12/31/2012
68. The JPB Foundation(NY)	1,096,930,211	12/31/2012
69. The Anschutz Foundation (CO)	1,066,522,739	11/30/2012
70. Foundation For The Carolinas (NC)	1,016,512,373	12/31/2012
71. Bat Hanadiv Foundation No. 3 (NY)	998,031,857	12/31/2012
72. Communities Foundation of Texas, Inc. (TX)	982,331,000	06/30/2013

73.	The Ahmanson Foundation (CA)	978,757,893	10/31/2012
74.	Cummings Foundation, Inc. (MA)	978,394,250	12/31/2012
75.	Shimon ben Joseph Foundation (CA)	973,736,964	12/31/2012
76.	The Broad Art Foundation (CA)	937,124,622	12/31/2012
77.	The Pittsburgh Foundation (PA)	905,146,642	12/31/2012
78.	Boston Foundation, Inc. (MA)	896,216,000	06/30/2013
79.	The J. E. and L. E. Mabee Foundation, Inc. (OK)	881,428,547	08/31/2013
80.	The Edna McConnell Clark Foundation (NY)	874,648,385	09/30/2012
81.	Druckenmiller Foundation (NY)	866,525,510	11/30/2012
82.	M. J. Murdock Charitable Trust (WA)	863,986,859	12/31/2012
83.	The California Wellness Foundation(CA)	847,982,323	12/31/2012
84.	The Joyce Foundation (IL)	832,164,870	12/31/2012
85.	Hall Family Foundation (MO)	822,884,571	12/31/2012
86.	Surdna Foundation, Inc. (NY)	814,855,442	06/30/2012
87.	Hartford Foundation for Public Giving (CT)	810,709,993	12/31/2012
88.	The Michael and Susan Dell Foundation (TX)	803,631,256	12/31/2012
89.	Robertson Foundation (NY)	801,679,030	11/30/2012
90.	Rockefeller Brothers Fund, Inc. (NY)	800,956,943	12/31/2012
91.	Otto Bremer Foundation (MN)	795,565,635	12/31/2012
92.	The Community Foundation for Greater Atlanta (GA)	793,327,000	12/31/2012
93.	Bush Foundation (MN)	780,000,000	12/31/2012
94.	The Freedom Forum, Inc. (DC)	765,567,826	12/31/2012
95.	The Henry Luce Foundation, Inc. (NY)	764,393,011	12/31/2012
96.	The ZOOM Foundation (CT)	738,246,659	06/30/2013
97.	The Morris and Gwendolyn Cafritz Foundation (DC)	728,428,540	04/30/2013
98.	Engelstad Family Foundation (NV)	728,328,702	12/31/2012
99.	Tosa Foundation (CA)	727,037,004	12/31/2012

100. The Ford Family Foundation (OR)   721,115,314 12/31/2012

Source: The Foundation Center
http://foundationcenter.org/findfunders/topfunders/top100assets.html

www.ingramcontent.com/pod-product-compliance
Lightning Source LLC
Chambersburg PA
CBHW081514200326
41518CB00015B/2495